TRANSATLANTIC FLIGHT

A Picture History
1873-1939

JOSHUA STOFF

DOVER PUBLICATIONS, INC.
MINEOLA, NEW YORK

To Jill,
best friend forever,
and for Matthew and Tyler,
the lights of our lives.

Nothing first without a dream.

Copyright

Copyright © 2000 by Joshua Stoff
All rights reserved under Pan American and International Copyright Conventions.

Published in Canada by General Publishing Company, Ltd., 30 Lesmill Road, Don Mills, Toronto, Ontario.

Bibliographical Note

Transatlantic Flight: A Picture History, 1873–1939 is a new work, first published by Dover Publications, Inc., in 2000.

Library of Congress Cataloging-in-Publication Data

Stoff, Joshua.
    Transatlantic flight : a picture history, 1873–1939 / Joshua Stoff.
        p. cm.
    ISBN 0-486-40727-6 (pbk.)
    1. Transatlantic flights—History—Sources. 2. Airplanes—Pictorial works. 3. Aeronautics—Pictorial works. I. Title.
TL531 .S76 2000
629.13'0911—dc21

00-031612

Book design by Carol Belanger Grafton

Manufactured in the United States of America
Dover Publications, Inc., 31 East 2nd Street, Mineola, N.Y. 11501

CONTENTS

PHOTO CREDITS

These institutions have generously supplied the photographs for this book. When the page numbers are not followed by such directions as top and bottom, it is understood that the credit applies to all the photographs on the page.

Cradle of Aviation Museum, Mitchel Field, Garden City, N.Y.: pages 1, 2, 3, 5(bottom), 6, 7, 10, 11(top), 13(top left), 18, 20, 21(bottom), 22(top), 23, 24, 25(top & bottom), 26(top), 29(top), 31(bottom), 32, 33, 35, 36, 37, 38, 39, 40, 41(top), 42, 43(bottom), 44, 45(top), 54(bottom), 58(top). 59, 62, 63, 64, 66(top), 67, 68(top), 69, 70, 71, 72, 73, 74(top), 76, 81, 82(top right), 83(bottom), 87, 88(bottom), 89, 90, 91, 93(bottom), 98(bottom), 103(top), 105, 106, 107, 108, 109, 110, 111, 112, 113, 114, 115, 116

National Air & Space Museum, Smithsonian Institution, Washington, D.C.: pages 4, 5(top & right), 8, 9, 11(bottom), 12(top), 13(top right), 14(top), 15, 16, 17, 19, 21(top), 22(bottom), 25(middle), 26(bottom), 27m 28, 29(bottom), 31(top), 34, 41(bottom), 43(top), 45(bottom), 46, 47, 49, 50, 52, 53(bottom), 54(top) 55, 56, 57, 58(bottom), 60, 61, 65, 66(bottom), 68(bottom), 74(bottom), 75, 77, 78, 79, 80, 82(top right & bottom), 83(top), 84, 85, 86, 88(top), 92(bottom), 93(top), 94, 95, 96, 97, 98(top), 100, 101, 102, 103(bottom), 104

National Aviation Museum, Ottawa, Ontario, Canada: 12(bottom), 13(bottom), 14(bottom), 48, 49(top), 51, 53(top)

EDO Corporation, 92(top)

INTRODUCTION

This book tells the story of the conquest of the Atlantic Ocean—the linking of the New World and the Old—by aircraft. Here is a survey of the many pioneering flights—both successful and failed—that were made by both Americans and Europeans, men and women, even some children (though not themselves at the controls), since the quest to fly across the North Atlantic began in 1873. This presentation hopes to capture, by words and photographs (many previously unpublished), an age when pilots took their wood-and-fabric airplanes into the skies, braving storms and darkness, when 200 miles per hour was considered an amazingly fast speed.

The sailing ship had been in existence for thousands of years before seamen were able to navigate safely across the North Atlantic. Yet, only sixteen years after the invention of the airplane aviators successfully crossed the water from North America to the British Isles. The big push had begun after World War I, as aviators vied with each other to conquer oceans and set new records. During the 1920s, optimism and confidence were in the air, even though the challenge posed by the wide Atlantic was not an easy one. Pilots were the great individualists, ready, willing, and able to strike out on their own to dare the unknown. They were often romantic, brave, headstrong, and, yes, reckless, even slightly mad. But the technology was there: Airplanes were capable—in theory, at least—of flying directly from North America to Europe. Flying the other way, from east to west against often daunting head winds, was a more doubtful proposition.

During this period people, especially Americans, were air-minded, eager to celebrate any new triumph in the skies. So it was that the unswerving determination and singularity of purpose embodied by young Charles Lindbergh fired the public's enthusiasm like nothing else. Lindy's careful planning, skillful navigation, and above all the fact that he did what he set out to do—by himself—was enough to turn him into one of the great heroes of the 20th century. The excitement and hoopla came to Lindbergh—he did not seek it. This book not only captures the thrill of achievement and progress that accompanied his flight, but it also puts the man and his flight into proper historical perspective. He wasn't the first or last to fly across the great ocean, but he was surely the most memorable.

Although this book captures the color, the flavor, and the triumphs of early aviation, its focus is squarely on the North Atlantic. This crossing was the one that had the most impact around the world because it linked the United States and Europe, where the big-city newspapers and other publicity machines were capable of turning unknowns into heroes. Flights across the South Atlantic were not covered nearly as much, and this emphasis, or lack thereof, is echoed on these pages. The availability of photographs has had no small influence on our coverage as well. Flights that took off from New York or London or Paris attracted far more reporters and photographers than those from smaller cities.

By 1939 the pioneering period of Atlantic flight was over. Regular airline service had begun, and the giant, luxurious airliners were attracting passengers in ever greater numbers. Today, over sixty years later, transatlantic air travel is routine. News is made only when something goes wrong with a flight. So, the next time you are sitting in a jumbo jet cruising over the Atlantic at more than 600 miles per hour, give a thought to the Atlantic pioneers—those who made it and those who did not. Their stories are told in these pages. You would not be flying the Atlantic today had so many brave men and women not been determined to be among the first to make the long and perilous journey on their own.

LIGHTER-THAN-AIR ATTEMPTS

The leading American balloonist of the 19th century, John Wise, dreamed of one day establishing regular aerial service between the U.S. and Europe. He designed a balloon especially for the journey, hung a lifeboat below the "basket," and named his ship *Atlantic* **(left)**. On July 1, 1859, Wise set out on a trial flight from St. Louis, Mo., with two passengers. They covered about 800 miles in twenty hours before crashing into a forest near Henderson, in northern New York **(below)**. All on board survived, but the aircraft was ruined.

Thaddeus Lowe, who later became famous for his aerial observation missions during the Civil War, in 1859 built a giant balloon rugged enough for the transatlantic journey. It was 200 feet high, had a large windowed gondola, and carried a steam-powered lifeboat underneath **(above)**. Lowe planned to fly his *City of New York* across the Atlantic, but the magnificent balloon was destroyed by a strong gust of wind just as it got off the ground for a test flight in Philadelphia **(below)**.

After the Civil War John Wise returned to his dream of becoming the first man to fly across the Atlantic Ocean. Sponsored by a New York tabloid, the *Daily Graphic,* Wise built a mammoth balloon with an inflation capacity of 400,00 cubic feet and with a gondola two stories high. An artist of the day pictured the cabin in a cutout view **(above, left)**. Wise backed out of the project when the newspaper proved more interested in self-promotion than in providing for a safe flight. A younger balloonist, Washington Donaldson **(above, right)**, took his place and set off from a field on Long Island, October 6, 1873. The somewhat unwieldy craft cruised smoothly over Long Island Sound **(right)** before running into a violent storm in Connecticut. The balloon crashed into a tree, but the crew was able to scramble down a rope to safety.

The technology of lighter-than-air flying ships changed dramatically in 1900, when the German Count Ferdinand von Zeppelin introduced his new aircraft, with its aerodynamic cigar shape and on-board engine. Similar ships were soon built in the U.S. One of them, the *America,* was bought by an entrepreneur named Walter Wellman **(left)** after it had failed in a flight to the North Pole. The engine room and the ship's bridge were slung under the balloon, along with a lifeboat **(middle)**. Wellman, posing here with his crew **(bottom)**, added a device he called an equilibriator, a weighted line to drag through the ocean waters in order to maintain the airship at a steady altitude.

With the sponsorship of several newspapers, Wellman and a crew of five took off from Atlantic City on October 15, 1910. Engine failure and other problems plagued the flight almost from the outset, but the aeronauts stayed the course for 71.5 hours and 1,008 miles. Finally, they spotted a potential rescuer, the steamship *Trent*, and brought their craft down for an ocean landing. Someone aboard the ship photographed the giant ship **(above)** before all the men were taken on board lifeboats **(right)**. Brought back to New York, they enjoyed a heroes' welcome. Meanwhile the *America* continued to drift to the northeast, and was never seen again.

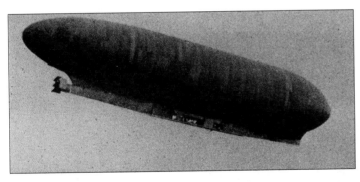

The chief engineer of Wellman's flight, Melvin Vaniman, refused to concede defeat and convinced the Goodyear Tire & Rubber Company to build America's largest dirigible, the three-engine *Akron*, to make the transatlantic trip **(above)**. Test flights went well, and Vaniman and his crew soon took off for Europe from Atlantic City. After fifteen minutes in the air, and still visible to the crowd of 3,000 well-wishers on the ground, the *Akron* exploded in a flash of fire and smoke. All five crew members perished, the first casualties in the war for transatlantic air superiority.

THE U.S. NAVY SUCCEEDS

In 1913 Lord Northcliffe, owner of the British newspaper the *Daily Mail*, offered a prize of £10,000 (equal to $50,000 then, to about $1 million in the year 2000) for the first successful transatlantic flight to or from Great Britain. The Curtiss Company responded to the challenge by building the largest flying boat of the day, the Model H, named *America*. Rodman Wanamaker, heir to a department-store fortune, was a major sponsor. The new airship, seen here on calm lake waters (**above**), was originally powered by two 90-hp Curtiss engines and equipped with a closed cabin for the crew on the long flight. The craft was launched June 22, 1914, in Hammondsport, New York; in this vintage photograph (**below**) the pilot, Lieutenant J.C. Porte, is on the left, and aviation pioneer Glenn Curtiss is next to Katherine Masson, who holds the traditional bottle of champagne.

The first test flight, from Lake Keuka, was witnessed by a small crowd of enthusiasts **(above)**. The *America* was a huge airplane for its time, as can be seen from the photographic comparison with the "standard hydro" at the right **(below)**. The photo was taken after the addition of a third engine, deemed necessary because the two engines did not supply enough power to lift the heavy fuel supply needed for the 3,000-mile trip across the ocean. The plan to take off from St. John's, Newfoundland, in August 1914 was put on hold after World War I broke out in Europe.

The famous Curtiss NC flying boats were the result of wartime design cooperation between the U.S. Navy and Curtiss (thus, the NC designation). The partners' goal was to manufacture an aircraft that could be flown across the ocean rather than being loaded aboard a ship that would be vulnerable to submarine and other attacks. The final product was a huge fourteen-foot flying boat with a wing span of 126 feet and powered by four 400-hp Liberty engines. Designed as combat aircraft, the NCs had gunners' compartments in the nose and under the top wing. When the war ended, the Navy decided to have three of the big boats, NC-1, NC-3, and NC-4, flown across the Atlantic, not for the Northcliffe prize but for prestige, both for the Navy and for the U.S. Here the crews are posed in front of the NC-1 at their home base, the Rockaway (N.Y.) Naval Air Station **(opposite, top)**. As part of the intense testing of the aircraft, the NC-1 is shown taxiing on Jamaica Bay **(opposite, bottom)**. On November 27, 1918, this aircraft carried a record fifty-one people aloft. The ships began their flight across the Atlantic on May 8, 1919, when they left Rockaway en route to Newfoundland, 950 miles away. This rare aerial photograph shows the NC-4 over the ocean, near Rockaway **(above)**.

The NCs all eventually made it to Trepassey Bay, Newfoundland, then, after last-minute checks, took off together across the Atlantic on May 16. They all fought through bad weather over the North Atlantic during the 1,400-mile flight to the Azores. The NC-1 landed at sea just short of the islands, giving up because of worsening weather conditions and a very low fuel supply. The crew abandoned ship and were taken aboard a nearby Greek freighter. They tried to tow the aircraft to port, but it was too heavily damaged and eventually sank. NC-3 also ran into strong weather and was forced to make an emergency landing. Unable to get back into the air, the crew turned the airplane's nose into the wind and used its tail as a sail. After riding out the storm for sixty-two hours, they were able to turn on the engines and taxi into the harbor at Horta, a major port in the Azores, to repair their battered craft **(above)**.

The NC-4 managed to bore on, landing at Horta without significant damage after a flight lasting 19 hours, 23 minutes. The crew then flew to Lisbon on May 27, landing on the River Tagus amidst cannon salutes from anchored warships **(below)**. Lt. Cmdr. Albert C. Read radioed his superiors, "We are safely on the other side of the pond. The job is finished."

All crew members of the three transatlantic aircraft were honored on their return to the U.S. **(left)**. In the first row are, from the left, Lt. Cmdr. Albert C. Read (NC-4), Secretary of the Navy Josephus Daniels, Cmdr. John Towers (NC-3), Asst. Secretary of the Navy Franklin D. Roosevelt, and Lt. Cmdr. P.N. Dellinger (NC-1). The NC-4 crew is in the second row, in front of the crews of the NC-1 and NC-3.

As the NCs made final preparations for the cross-ocean trip, on May 15 the Naval Airship C-5 quietly took off from the naval air station at Montauk, Long Island. After the longest flight by a nonrigid airship to that date, she arrived at the jump-off point in Newfoundland. Crews tied her down securely **(below)**, but within hours a powerful gale tore her from the moorings. Unmanned, the big ship sailed out to sea and disappeared.

1919: First Nonstops

The first competitor for the *Daily Mail* prize was a British officer, Maj. J.C. Woods, who flew a Short Brothers airplane named the *Shamrock*. Woods attempted to make the crossing from east to west, taking off from Eastchurch, England, on April 18, 1919. Apparently, little preparation had been made for the flight, and plane and pilot were forced to quit over the Irish Sea, just twenty-two miles west of the coast of Wales. Woods was rescued, leaving his plane barely afloat **(left)**.

Several British aircraft firms entered planes in the transatlantic contest, banking on the fact that the winner would reap great rewards from the acclaim that would come to the winning aircraft. The first to arrive at the preferred takeoff point in Newfoundland was a Sopwith single-engine biplane called the *Atlantic*. **(below)**. The upper part of this unique airplane's fuselage was designed to be used as a life raft in emergencies. Another unique feature was its adjustable landing gear, which could be dropped after takeoff to reduce weight and drag in the air.

Sopwith's most experienced test pilot, Harry Hawker **(above, left)**, and his navigator, Kenneth Mackenzie-Grieve, took off from Mount Pearl on May 18, 1919, just clearing the trees at the end of the runway. Nothing more was heard from them, and the press assumed the worst—lost at sea. But on May 25 came word that a Danish freighter sailing without a radio had picked them up after the *Atlantic*'s radiator had overheated in mid-flight. The photograph **(above, right)** was taken before the *Atlantic* disappeared under the waves.

Also contending for the *Daily Mail*'s prize was another single-engine biplane, the *Raymor*, built by Martinsyde. The pilot, Freddie Raynham, and his navigator, when they saw the *Atlantic* get airborne, quickly prepared for takeoff from Quid Vidi, nearby **(below)**. A severe crosswind sheared off their landing gear, however, and the *Raymor* went nose-down before takeoff. Both men were lucky and survived the crash.

Meanwhile, Captain John Alcock, at right **(opposite, top)**, an R.A.F. ace from World War I, and his navigator, Arthur Whitten Brown, at left, had arrived in Newfoundland to prepare for their flight in a Vickers Vimy, a fast new bomber. In an open field often swept by windy, wet weather, they unpacked, reassembled, and tested their aircraft **(opposite, bottom)**, then waited for favorable weather. Fourteen days after their arrival, on June 14, they took off **(above)** from the airstrip that had been used by Freddy Raynham. After a brief, reassuring radio transmission, they vanished into the mists of the North Atlantic. Nothing further was heard until the Vimy reappeared just inland from the Irish coast: Alcock and Brown had survived the 16-hour-and-28-minute flight to become the first to fly nonstop across the Atlantic.

The story they later told was one of heroism and uncommon skill, along with both good and bad luck. Early in the flight they had lost sight of the ocean in a fog bank, and then haze blocked out the sun. Finally, they became disoriented when they no longer could see the horizon, and the plane went into a spin. Alcock recovered and was able to pull up about 100 feet above the ocean. They pressed on until they spotted land, then put the plane down in a likely looking landing place that turned out to be a bog. The Vimy went nose-down (above), but Alcock and Brown had made it across the ocean and thus had won the prize. Later, in London, they were knighted by the king. Sir John Alcock died in a crash not a year later, but Sir Arthur Brown never flew again and lived on until 1948.

Among the disappointed left-behinds was a huge aircraft, a Handley-Page V-1500 bomber **(below)**, which had arrived in Newfoundland on May 10. She had a five-man crew, commanded by Admiral Mark Kerr, and a large support staff on the ground. Early test flights had revealed a problem with the aircraft's radiator, leading Kerr to suspend operations and await the arrival of a replacement from England. It came too late. The Vickers team had won the race, and Handley-Page turned its attention to attempting a New-York-to-Chicago flight. Problems continued, however, and on that flight the V-1500 was finally destroyed in a forced landing on a racetrack in Cleveland; all members of the crew survived.

The third successful flight across the Atlantic was made by the R-34, a rigid airship built for the British military **(opposite, top)**. A giant at 641 feet long and powered by five 250-hp Sunbeam engines in the rear gondola **(opposite, bottom)**, the R-34 left East Fortune, Scotland, on July 2, en route to New York. The R-34 maintained radio contact throughout her comparatively uneventful flight, reporting mid-flight that strong head winds made it heavy going. It was possible that fuel would run out before they reached North America. The winds shifted, however, and the great ship arrived over Long Island **(above)** after a 3,200-mile journey that took 108 hours and 12 minutes. Maj. J.M. Pritchard parachuted down onto Roosevelt Field and helped to organize the landing party.

The crew, commanded by Maj. G.H. Scott **(left)**, received a hero's welcome and then, after a brief layover, took the R-34 aloft on July 9 and arrived at Pulham, England, 75 hours and 3 minutes later. The first round-trip flight across the Atlantic was a success. Just over a year later the R-34 was badly damaged when she ran into a hill on a flight in Yorkshire; deemed not worth repairing, the historic craft was consigned to the scrap heap.

WORLD CRUISERS

The next challenge for military air power was to fly around the world. The U.S. War Department commissioned Douglas Aircraft of California to build four high-performance airplanes based on an existing design for torpedo bombers. The Douglas World Cruisers (DWCs) were biplanes that had fifty-foot wing spans and were powered by 400-hp Liberty engines. DWC-4, the *New Orleans,* was photographed during its stay at Mitchel Field, on Long Island **(above)**.

The other three aircraft were *Seattle*, *Boston*, and *Chicago*, all named to more or less represent four corners of the United States, and each carried a pilot and a mechanic. Six of the world fliers, all members of the U.S. Air Service, gathered for a group photo before departure **(above)**: from the left, Sgt. H.H. Ogden, Lt. Leslie Arnold, Lt. Leigh Wade, Lt. Lowell Smith, Maj. Frederick Martin, and Sgt. Alva Harvey. The aircraft attracted large crowds at Clover Field, California **(below)**, near Santa Monica, before leaving for Seattle, where they were given an official send-off on April 6, 1924. They headed north to Alaska, on the first leg of the journey, and ran into their first mishap. The *Seattle*, flown by Maj. Martin, crashed into a mountainside; given up for lost, pilot and mechanic surprised everyone by walking out of the wilderness in good shape ten days later.

Meanwhile the three surviving craft headed west, to Japan, China, India, Turkey, and into the heart of Europe. The World Cruisers attracted crowds of aviation enthusiasts when they landed in France in July **(above)**. Continuing their journey, the aircraft headed across France and out over the Atlantic. There, the *Boston* lost oil pressure and was forced to land at sea. The crew was rescued, but when a hoist lifting the aircraft onto the deck of a U.S. Navy cruiser gave way, it capsized and sank **(below)**.

The other airplanes continued to Iceland, where the *New Orleans* was photographed, on floats, tied up at Reykjavik **(above)**. The DWCs were there at the same time as another round-the-world pilot, Lt. Antonio Locatelli of the Italian Air Service, in his Dornier Wal flying boat. Locatelli took off with the American planes as they headed west, toward Greenland, but his engine soon failed. He was rescued after spending three days bobbing in the ocean. Joined by *Boston 2,* the round-the-worlders continued to the U.S., where they were photographed on their approach to Mitchel Field **(below)**. They completed their historic trip where it had officially begun, in Seattle.

THE ORTEIG PRIZE

French-born New York hotel owner Raymond Orteig **(right)** startled the aviation world in 1919 with his offer of $25,000 prize for the first nonstop flight between New York and Paris. Not until about six years later did improved technology make such a flight feasible. In 1925 World War I ace Rene Fonck received the backing of some French businessmen and commissioned American aircraft maker Igor Sikorsky to build an aircraft capable of making the dangerous journey (twice as long as Alcock and Brown's 1919 flight). A large biplane, the S-35, powered by three French-built Jupiter 425-hp engines, was built at Roosevelt Field, Long Island. By mid-September, the plane was ready to go **(below)**.

Preparations for the flight were followed by an eager public. The many publicity photos included a pose with a comely young flapper **(right)** and a wide-angle shot showing the drums full of the fuel needed for the flight **(middle)**—ultimately, the plane took on over 15,000 pounds of gas and oil. On September 20, 1926, Fonck climbed aboard the S-35 with a crew of three: Lt. Lawrence Curtin, USN, Charles Clavier, and Jacob Islamoff. The big craft trundled down the mile-long runway but failed to lift off; it cartwheeled into a gulley at the end of the runway, and seven and one half tons of fuel exploded in flames. Fonck and Curtin were thrown clear and survived, but Clavier and Islamoff died in the crash. The remains of the aircraft **(bottom)** are mute evidence of the force of the impact and subsequent fire.

Fearless, like most aviation pioneers, Fonck persuaded Sikorsky to begin work on a new, improved aircraft, the S-37 *Ville de Paris*. The plane was ready late in 1927 **(above)**, but dreams of glory were shattered by the successful flights by Lindbergh, Byrd, and Chamberlin.

After the failure of Fonck's S-35, and before Lindbergh's flight, the leading candidates to win the Orteig prize appeared to be Lt. Cmdr. Noel Davis and his copilot, Stanton Wooster. They are seen here inspecting their plane, a Keystone Pathfinder bomber **(below)**; Davis is at the left. The aircraft was named the *American Legion* in honor of their war veteran sponsors.

Their base of operations was Langley Field in Virginia, where the pilots made a number of test flights **(above)**. Early on the morning of April 26, 1927, Davis and Wooster took off on one last test, with the plane carrying a full load, including 17,000 pounds of fuel. The *American Legion* got off the ground but in veering away from a stand of trees went nose-down and crashed in a nearby marsh **(below)**. Both Davis and Wooster lost their lives.

A bemedalled Charles Nungesser was among the greatest of the heroes to survive the 1916-1918 air war between France and Germany **(left)**. Like a number of pioneering aviators, he had a well-developed ego and headstrong opinions. Thus his French compatriots were not particularly surprised when he decided to compete for the Orteig prize by flying from Paris to New York. Yes, he would have to fight headwinds, but his aircraft, a Levavasseur PL-8 biplane with a single, water-cooled engine and an open cockpit, was tough and powerful, having been built for the French navy **(middle)**. It was capable of carrying twice as much fuel as most other planes, and its heavy landing gear **(bottom)** was rigged so that it could be detached after takeoff, thus eliminating several hundred pounds of dragging weight.

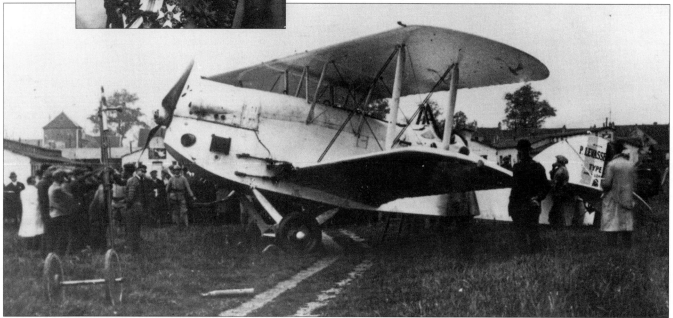

As for arrival in New York, Nungesser planned to make a dramatic pancake landing in the harbor—in the shadow of the great French gift to America, the Statue of Liberty. Waiting for favorable weather, Nungesser and his navigator, eyepatch-wearing Capt. Francois Coli, posed in their plane, *L'Oiseau Blanc* ("The White Bird"), which carried the same sinister insignia as all the planes Nungesser had flown against the Germans in World War I **(top)**. On May 8, 1927, at 5:17 A.M., a large crowd cheered as Nungesser and Coli became the first Orteig contestants to get their fuel-laden plane off the ground. The last photograph of the plane was taken after it had cleared the French coast and dropped its landing gear **(bottom)**. Nothing more was heard of the aircraft after it cleared the Irish coasts but there came ominous reports that head winds over the Atlantic were running about 25 mph. At that rate *L'Oiseau Blanc* would run out of fuel about 400 miles short of North America. Dire predictions about the fate of plane and crew proved to be accurate: The intrepid Frenchmen were never seen again, the fifth and sixth casualties in the transatlantic race.

THE LONE EAGLE

On a night flight in 1926 the idea came to Charles Lindbergh, a young airmail pilot, that he could fly nonstop from New York all the way to Paris if he had the right aircraft. Lindy thought a single-engine plane could do it—a more powerful three-engine craft had three times the chance of crippling engine failure—and that he could find his way without a navigator, thus saving weight and space for additional fuel. He was turned down by the premier maker of long-distance planes, Bellanca, so he turned to the small Ryan Company of San Diego, manufacturers of mail planes. Ryan was willing to make an aircraft to Lindbergh's specifications for the $25,000 the young pilot had been able to raise from a group of businessmen in St. Louis. The photo of the Wright J5 engine chosen by Lindbergh **(above)** was taken during the time his plane was under construction.

This publicity photo (above) was taken in exchange for a supply of fuel. Lindbergh towers above Donald Hall, Ryan's chief engineer, to his left, and others on the site. Among the plane's features built to Lindy's specifications was the instrument panel (left). Top center is the earth inductor compass, which provided a more accurate reading than a magnetic compass. The altimeter, airspeed indicator, and clock are at the right. The square opening at the left is for the periscope; the lever next to it slides the periscope in and out. The T-shaped instrument in the lower center is basically a level that shows the aircraft's attitude—the simulated horizon had not yet been invented.

On May 10, 1927, the newly named *Spirit of St. Louis* took off from San Diego, headed east. Lindbergh landed first in St. Louis to greet his backers and other supporters, then flew on to New York and Curtiss Field on Long Island. The American public had become fascinated with the modest loner they came to know as Lindy, despite his being derided by some members of the press as the "Flying Fool." He wasn't rich or flamboyant and did not have a large publicity organization behind him. Yet, Lindbergh and his plane were routinely surrounded by members of the press and public whenever either emerged from the hangar at Curtiss Field **(above)**.

Transatlantic rivals Richard E. Byrd and Clarence Chamberlin were also at Curtiss, waiting for good weather for takeoff. Here Byrd, with his arm still in the cast put on after a test flight crash, and Chamberlin meet Lindbergh in the *Spirit's* hangar **(opposite)**.

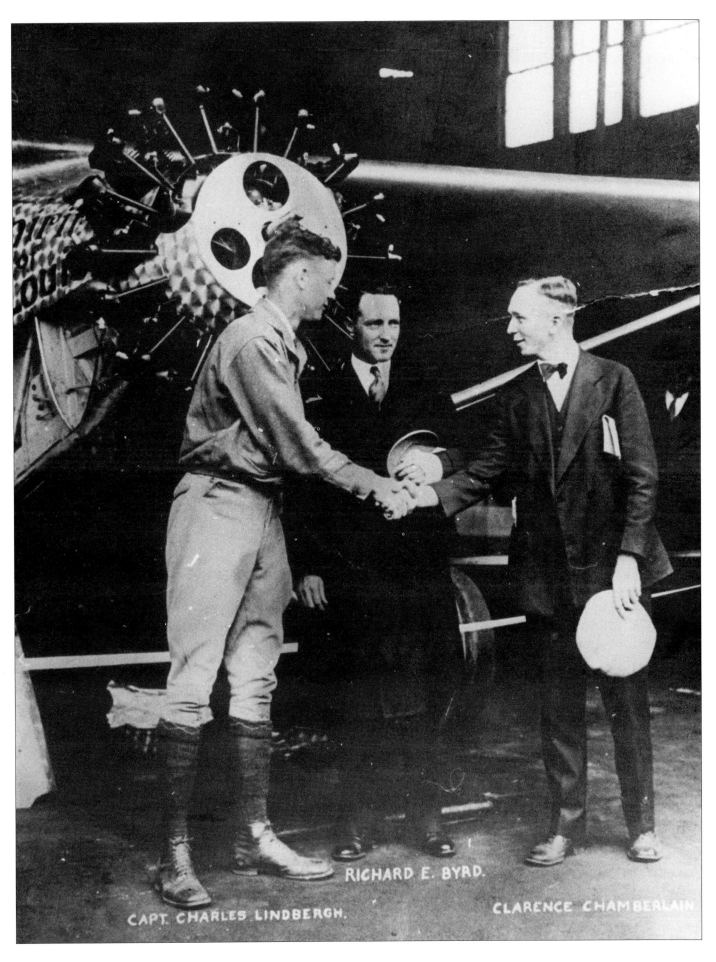

CAPT. CHARLES LINDBERGH.   RICHARD E. BYRD.   CLARENCE CHAMBERLAIN

During the week Lindbergh was at Curtiss Field he made several test flights to check out his new compass and carburetor heater. This commercial photo **(above)** was taken before the May 14th flight, when Lindbergh established optimum fuel mixture settings with the help of Wright engineers. About 7 A.M. on May 20, 1927, the *Spirit,* checked out and ready to fly, sits at the end of the runway at Roosevelt Field **(below).** Lindbergh had moved the plane from neighboring Curtiss Field to take advantage of Roosevelt's mile-long runway. The sky is drizzly and overcast, the field is muddy. The ground crew has covered the engine with a blanket to keep out the dampness.

The last of the 450 gallons of fuel has been put aboard by hand, from five-gallon tanks. Fully loaded, the plane weighs about 2 1/2 tons. At around 7:40 Lindbergh puts on his leather flying suit (above). The *Spirit of St. Louis* is all ready. A crowd of around 150 people watches as Lindbergh climbs into the cockpit, buckles his safety belt, pulls down his goggles, and peers out the left window. The crowd moves away, to make room for the plane to taxi (below).

Lindbergh waves away the chocks and opens the engine full throttle. Mechanics and spectators rush in and push on the wing struts to get the heavy plane moving **(above)**. The *Spirit* gains speed, then lifts off and sinks back to the runway before gaining enough flying speed to clear the trees and utility wires at the end of the runway. Later that day, Lindbergh was spotted passing over Newfoundland, and then there was no news for sixteen hours. He carried no radio in order to diminish the plane's weight.

At 10:24 P.M., May 21, 1927, Lindbergh landed at LeBourget Airfield outside Paris. Exhausted by his thirty-three-and-one-half-hour flight, he was shocked to see 100,000 cheering Frenchmen streaming across the field **(opposite, top)**. Ever naive, he had no idea if anyone at all would be at the airport to greet him. Lindbergh was now a hero throughout the world. Huge crowds followed his every move. Among the many awards Lindy received was the gold medal of the National Geographic Society, which was presented to him by President Calvin Coolidge in November 1927 **(opposite, bottom)**. Then and in subsequent years Lindbergh saw himself less as a pioneer than as a missionary bringing the word to people in the U.S. and the rest of the world of the limitless possibilities of aviation. (He was also an early advocate of rocketry and space travel.)

NEXT ACROSS

Despite Lindbergh's world-shaking success, many of the original competitors for the Orteig prize did not give up. Clarence Chamberlin, posing here with his would-be navigator Lloyd Bertaud and aircraft designer Giuseppe Bellanca **(above)**, was certainly not happy when he saw Lindbergh take off on May 20. His own plane, a Wright-powered Bellanca named *Columbia*, was also at Roosevelt Field. NEW YORK—PARIS was emblazoned on its fuselage, along with a credit line, "Auspices Brooklyn Chamber of Commerce" **(opposite, top)**. The smallest of the transatlantic contenders, it was nevertheless considered a favorite because the shape of its wing, fuselage, and struts provided lift to get the plane airborne even with an extra-heavy load. Chamberlin's *Columbia* was ready for flight but had been grounded by a court order obtained by Bertaud, who believed he had been illegally dropped from the flight. When the order was lifted on June 4, the plane's elusive owner, Charles Levine, arrived at the airfield. He and Chamberlin shook hands before takeoff **(opposite, bottom)**.

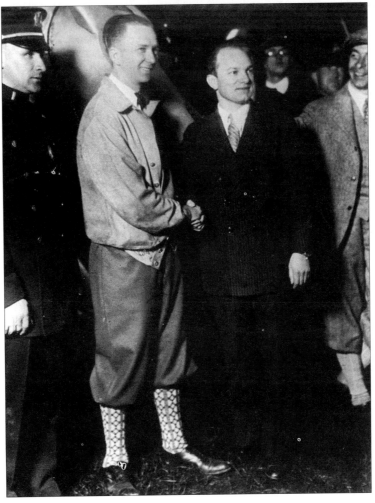

The plane taxied down the same runway that had been used by the *Spirit* (**above**) and successfully took off, headed east toward "anyplace in Europe." The *Columbia* maintained a steady course over open water (**opposite, top**) and kept going over the European land mass. Finally running out of fuel over Germany, Chamberlin and Levine landed in a wheatfield about 100 miles short of Berlin. The 43-hour flight had covered 3,911 miles, about 300 miles more than Lindbergh's. Just to the left of the German policeman looking at the plane can be seen how the word PARIS had been obliterated before the plane left New York (**opposite, bottom**).

In the fall of 1928 Charles Levine's *Columbia* was once again poised at Roosevelt Field to make another ocean crossing. This time the destination was Rome, and the pilots were Roger Q. Williams (left) and Capt. Pietro Bonelli **(right)**. Before takeoff, as a precaution against ice buildup, they coated the plane's wing with paraffin wax. But the wax had the unfortunate effect of diminishing the *Columbia's* lift , and the ship came back to earth on a golf course just a mile east of the airfield. The landing gear was wiped out.

Undeterred, Levine had the plane repaired and tested again in flight **(above)**. In 1930 he leased it to Capt. J. Errol Boyd of the Royal Canadian Flying Corps. who renamed it the *Maple Leaf*. With Harry Connor of the U.S. Navy as navigator, Boyd took off from Harbour Grace, Newfoundland, on October 9, 1930, bound for London. A clogged fuel line forced them to land in the Isles of Scilly, just off Land's End, England. The next day they flew on to London, where the Bellanca was feted as the only airplane to fly across the Atlantic twice.

Last of the Orteig competitors to get off the ground was Cmdr. Richard E. Byrd, USN, seen here at Roosevelt Field with his crew **(left)**: from left, Richard Acosta, Byrd, George Noville, and Bernt Balchen, who gained fame as Byrd's chief pilot in the Antarctic. Their plane was a Fokker trimotor christened *America* in a ceremony at Roosevelt Field **(below)**.

Byrd had a special down-sloping ramp built **(above)** to help them gain speed at takeoff **(opposite, top)**. Over the Atlantic the flight ran into the worst weather faced by any of the transatlantic pilots. Fortunately, the *America* was equipped with the best instruments available at the time. There was so much fog above Newfoundland that they never caught sight of land, and they ran into rain, turbulence, ice, and thick clouds over the storm-tossed North Atlantic. Despite the obstacles they made it to France—but then they were unable to find their way to Paris. When they began to run out of fuel, Balchen became the first pilot ever to ditch a big trimotor. He executed a perfect emergency landing just off the beach at Ver-Sur-Mer in Brittany **(opposite, bottom)**. Leaving their aircraft in the surf, the dazed crew made their way ashore in a rubber raft. Thus, within three weeks three American airplanes had crossed the Atlantic successfully.

LOST AT SEA

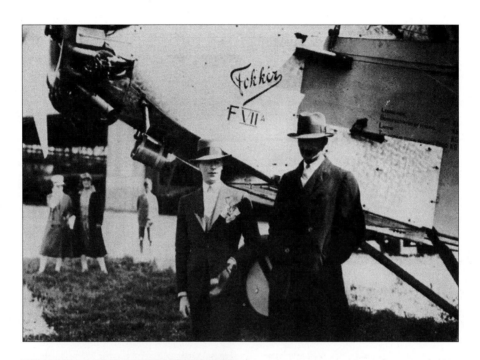

Two English aviators had also entered the transatlantic race in 1927 **(above)**. Leslie Hamilton, at left, and Fred Minchin, at right, were hired by Princess Anne Lowenstein-Wertheim **(left)**, who wanted to be the first woman to cross the Atlantic in an airplane. The threesome set off in a Fokker F-7 named *St. Raphael* on August 31, 1927. They left from Salisbury, England, bound for Ottawa, Canada. The plane was spotted once, by a freighter in mid-ocean, but was never seen again. All hands were lost at sea.

Lloyd Bertaud, the spurned navigator who had held up Chamberlin's flight, soon joined another transatlantic team, this one hoping to fly from New York to Rome. Sponsored by William Randolph Hearst as a publicity stunt for his newspapers, the flight was also to be made in a Fokker F-7, this one named *Old Glory*. At the plant in New Jersey where the Fokker was being fitted out, navigator James Hill (left) and pilot Bertaud checked it out with Anthony Fokker, leaning on the engine **(opposite, top)**. Joined by newspaper editor Philip Payne, Bertaud and Hill took off from the hard-packed sand of Old Orchard Beach, Maine, on September 6 **(opposite, bottom)**. Two SOS signals were heard from *Old Glory* on September 7, but nothing further was reported until a freighter sighted the wreckage floating 600 miles off Newfoundland. Hearst sent his condolences to the bereaved families.

Canadians also joined the 1927 race, as the Carling Brewery offered a prize of $25,000 for the first flight from London, Ontario, to London, England. The plane was a Stinson Detroiter named *Sir John Carling* **(above)**, flown by Capt. Terence Tully, left, and Lt. James Metcalf, right. They took off from Harbour Grace, Newfoundland, on September 7 **(below)**. But luck ran against them, and Tully and Metcalf disappeared into the vast open water of the North Atlantic.

At the same time another Stinson Detroiter was set to fly from Windsor, Ontario, to Windsor, England. Pilots Clarence Schiller and Phil Wood had brought their *Royal Windsor*—so named by the businessmen from Windsor who sponsored the flight—to the jump-off point at Harbour Grace **(top)**. When they learned that both *Old Glory* and *Sir John Carling* appeared to be lost at sea, they decided to abandon their own flight. Not so Mrs. Francis Grayson, a well-to-do realtor from Forest Hills, New York City, who was determined to be the first woman on a successful transatlantic flight. With backing from a Danish-American woman, Mrs. Aage Ancker, she engaged pilot Wilmer Stutz and navigator Bryce Goldsmith to fly a twin-engine Sikorsky S-38 amphibian she named *Dawn* **(middle)**.

In October the trio made three abortive takeoffs from Old Orchard Beach before Stutz quit, fearing the onset of harsh winter weather in the North Atlantic. Mrs. Grayson then hired a Norwegian pilot, Lt. Oskar Omdahl, veteran of three arctic flights. The two posed by their aircraft at Roosevelt Field, site of their takeoff on Christmas Eve, 1927 **(left)**. Mrs. Grayson and her crew of three were also lost at sea.

On the other side of the Atlantic, in Great Britain, an actress named Elsie Mackay **(right)**, daughter of a wealthy shipowner, had been nursing the same ambition as Mrs. Grayson. She gave Walter Hinchcliffe, a pilot for British Imperial Airways, $50,000 to buy himself a Stinson Detroiter and fly her across the Atlantic. Hinchcliffe was known for his skilled, intrepid airmanship, and for doing it with the use of only one eye. On March 12, 1928—too early in the year for them to have much of a chance of decent weather—they took off from Cranwell Military Aerodrome. They, too, fell victim to the unforgiving Atlantic. Another Stinson Detroiter, named *Greater Rockford* and piloted by ex-barnstormers Bert Hassell and Parker Cramer, took off from Rockford, Ill., after a rousing send-off on July 26, 1928 **(below)**. With the backing of local businessmen, they hoped to make a pioneering flight from the American Midwest to northern Europe via the Great Circle route. All went well until they were unable to find one of their stopover points, a landing field on Greenland. Running out of fuel, they had to land on Greenland's forbidding icecap—the first ever to accomplish this feat. Hassell and Cramer set out to find help and managed to survive for two weeks before local Eskimos notified a rescue party of their whereabouts. Remarkably, their plane was recovered in 1969 and was made flyable once again.

On October 9, 1928, a retired Royal Navy officer named H.C. MacDonald began a flight from Harbour Grace, Newfoundland, to Ireland. His DeHavilland Gypsy Moth was one of the smallest planes to attempt the long flight **(above)**. MacDonald met good weather at first, and his aircraft was sighted by a freighter about 700 miles out at sea. But that was the last anyone ever saw of MacDonald and his little biplane.

The transatlantic attempt with the least chance of success was probably the one made by Urban Diteman, a cattle rancher from Billings, Montana **(left)**. Leaving his family behind, Diteman flew across the country to Harbour Grace in the small, open cockpit Barling monoplane he used to get around his big ranch. He filed a flight plan for New York, but when he took off on October 22, he headed east, out to sea. Like many others, he disappeared without a trace.

Mrs. Beryl Hart was a well-off New Yorker who also wanted to be the first woman to make the transatlantic flight. She and her flight instructor, William MacLaren, pausing to pose before flight **(right)**, planned what they thought would be the easy way over. They took off from North Beach in Queens, New York, on January 3, 1931, and headed southeast, toward Bermuda. So confident of success were they that they carried 200 pounds of paid cargo in the hold of their float-equipped Bellanca, the *Tradewind*. Bad weather forced them to land in Virginia, but they soon resumed their journey and landed safely in Bermuda. After a few days' rest, on January 10 they took off and headed east. Not far off Bermuda they ran into a strong Northeast storm—and oblivion.

In Germany twenty-one-year-old Willi Rodi bought a Junkers W33 and prepared for his own west-to-east transatlantic journey. Teamed up with Christian Johannson and Fernando Viega, he took off in the Junkers, which he named *Esa* for his bride, from Junco do Sol, Portugal, on September 13, 1931. They had no radio for communication but were sighted passing over the Azores. The engine soon started missing, and they were forced to fly at full throttle, thus using more fuel than anticipated. Ultimately, they ran out of gas and landed in the ocean ninety-two miles short of Newfoundland. They scrambled out of the cockpit onto the wing and waited for the plane to sink. But it floated remarkably well, and they were able to subsist for a week on some mushy chocolate and water from the plane's radiator. On September 20 the forlorn trio was rescued by the crew of a Norwegian freighter, who had spotted them on the aircraft's roof **(above)**. This photo was taken from the freighter in a relatively calm sea just before the rescue.

A Norwegian immigrant named John Bochkon, who had settled in Vermont, was another entrant in the transatlantic derby. He convinced some businessmen in Barre and Montpelier, Vermont, to gain public notice around the world for the local quarries by sponsoring his flight to Oslo, Norway. They agreed, and his plane, the *Green Mt. Boy*, carried the slogan "Granite Center of the World." With barnstormer Clyde Lee, at right **(above)**, Bochkon took off from Harbour Grace in excellent weather. Unfortunately, a storm developed at sea. Like so many others, these two aviators failed to reach land, and were never seen again.

Another flight that seemed more publicity stunt than anything else was organized by Leon Pisciuli, M.D., whose stated purpose was to observe the effect of extended flight on human beings. It took him four years to raise the money to buy a Bellanca suitable for the long journey. He named the aircraft *American Nurse* **(below)**. With pilot William Ulrich (right) Pisciuli took off from Floyd Bennett Field in Brooklyn, New York, on September 13, 1932. Also on the flight was a young nurse, Edna Newcomer (center), who was to assist Pisciuli with his scientific observations. The Bellanca was spotted en route by an ocean liner but then disappeared without a trace.

EAST TO WEST

After Lindbergh's sensational west-to-east flight, the French were anxious to claim some of the glory and honor by having the first successful Europe-to-America flight take off from their country. On September 2, 1927, a Farman biplane with twin engines back to back and named *L'Oiseau Bleu* ("The Bluebird") **(above)**, took off from Le Bourget with pilots Leon Givan and Pierre Corbu. They ran into extremely poor weather but persisted with their heavy load of fuel for four hours before giving up and returning to Paris.

The next month another French crew tried a different route across the ocean. Dieudonné Costes and Joseph LeBrix took off from the French colony of Senegal in their Breguet biplane **(right)**, which they named *Nungesser-Coli* in honor of their countrymen who had been lost at sea. They made the comparatively short hop across the South Atlantic safely, but without the great newspaper publicity machines in Paris and New York, and without the personal drama inherent in Lindbergh's solitary journey, the flight garnered little interest worldwide.

Meanwhile, in England, Frank Courtney **(above)** and F.M. Downer took off in a German-built Dornier Wal flying boat just one day after Givan and Corbu's attempt. They also ran into unfavorable weather and returned to base. Almost a year later, in August 1928, Courtney took off from Lisbon, Portugal, in the same aircraft **(below)** but with a new crew. Halfway across, the plane caught fire and they were forced to land in the ocean. Their radioed SOS was answered by a nearby liner, and all hands were soon rescued.

Germany also caught the transatlantic fever. Freed in 1926 from the restrictions imposed by the Treaty of Versailles, the Junkers works produced two special models of their new all-metal monoplane for the long ocean flight. The *Bremen* **(above)** was sponsored by the North German Lloyd steamship line, the *Europa* **(opposite, top)** by the Hearst newspapers. Hearst correspondent W.R. Knickerbocker, center, made the flight with Johann Risticz, at left, and Cornelius Edzard, at right **(opposite, bottom)**. The two planes set off at the same time but on different courses from Dessau, north of Liepzig, on August 15, 1927. The *Europa* ran into dense fog in the North Sea, turned back, and was badly damaged in an emergency landing. The *Bremen* made it to the open sea west of Ireland, but strong head-winds forced it to turn around, too.

Less than a year later, on April 12, 1928, the *Bremen* took off from Baldonnel Aerodrome near Dublin, with an Irishman, Maj. James Fitzmaurice, and the Germans Baron Von Huenefeld and Hermann Koehl on board. Head winds reduced their average ground speed to 56 mph, but they pressed on and, after turning away from a dense fog bank in Newfoundland, made an emergency landing on Greely Island off the coast of Labrador **(opposite, top)**. The plane's undercarriage was destroyed, making any further flight impossible, but their goal had been reached— the first east-to-west nonstop flight from Europe to North America. They were soon picked up by Admiral Byrd's trimotor and eventually made it to New York. There Koehl, Fitzmaurice, and Von Huenefeld, seen from left to right **(opposite, bottom)**, received a hero's welcome. The photo **(above)** is a street-side view of the classic New York ticker-tape parade of the sort that welcomed this trio, Lindbergh, and many other aviators of this era.

The French aviators Dieudonné Costes, at left, and Maurice Bellone, at right **(opposite, top)**, never gave up on their Paris-New York flight. On September 1, 1930, they left Le Bourget in their Breguet biplane, the *Question Mark* **(above)**, and completed a long (37 hours, 18 minutes) but successful flight. They flew over New York City **(opposite, middle)** before landing at Curtiss Field on Long Island **(opposite, bottom)**, where, away from the crowds, they were greeted by Lindbergh.

WOMEN CROSS THE SEA

Despite the disappearance at sea of several of the women seeking to fly across the Atlantic, others were quick to enter the contest. On October 11, 1927, student pilot Ruth Elder and her flight instructor, George Haldeman, took off from Roosevelt Field in their Stinson Detroiter, the *American Girl* (**opposite, top**). But their engine overheated just east of the Azores, and they were forced to ditch the Stinson. Soon picked up by a passing freighter, the glamorous Elder and the businesslike Haldeman were given a big welcome back home (**opposite, bottom**).

Germany's first licensed female pilot, Thea Rasche, won the backing of a wealthy American, Mrs. James Stillman for a transatlantic flight planned for June 1928. Here, from right to left, Rasche, Stillman, and navigator Ulrich Koenemann pose beside the Bellanca they named the *North Star* (**above**). Problems began when the plane was damaged on its takeoff from Harbour Grace, and eventually all parties abandoned the flight.

The woman who was to become one of the most famous aviators in history, Amelia Earhart **(above)**, began her public life as the first woman to make a successful transatlantic flight. Her opportunity originated in England, where Mrs. Frederick Guest bought Richard Byrd's Fokker Trimotor, renamed it the *Friendship* **(opposite, top)**, and engaged Bill Stultz as pilot and Slim Gordon as navigator to fly her across the Atlantic. Mrs. Guest's family had other ideas. Citing the numbers of women (and men) who had been lost at sea, they persuaded her not to make the flight. She then asked a friend, publisher G.P. Putnam, to look for a "suitable girl" as substitute. A young social worker in Boston, Amelia Earhart, was suggested, and passed on to Mrs. Guest by Putnam, who noted that she looked enough like Lindbergh to be his sister. After three failed takeoff attempts, Earhart and crew left Newfoundland on June 17, 1928. Twenty hours later they landed in the harbor of Burry Port, Wales. Gordon, Earhart, Stutz, and Guest, seen from left ro right **(opposite, bottom)**, were feted by the British, and Amelia Earhart became an instant celebrity. She went on to become an outstanding pilot in competitions, setting several speed records.

Another American, Ruth Nichols, had broken two women's flight records—transcontinental speed (1930) and altitude (1931)—before she borrowed a Lockheed Vega, named *Akita*, and flew to the jump-off point at St. John's, Newfoundland, on June 21, 1931 **(above)**. Unfortunately, in landing, she overshot the short St. John's runway and crashed into a hillside, breaking several bones. She remained in Newfoundland, still hoping to make the flight, but in October her plane was destroyed by fire, and her hopes for transatlantic fame and fortune went up in smoke.

A plucky, glamorous woman with solid experience as a bush pilot in Kenya, Beryl Markham **(right)**, was determined to be the first woman to make the difficult east-to-west transatlantic flight in her light plane, a Percival Gull. Despite strong head winds and generally poor weather, she took off from Abingdon, England, on September 4, 1936. She flew for nineteen hours through darkness and rain, with no communication with the outside world because she was not carrying a radio. Approaching Nova Scotia, her engine quit, possibly because of a clogged fuel line. Markham spotted a level field and glided down for a landing. The field proved to be a bog, however, and the plane nosed over in the soft mud **(below)**. Markham sustained some head injuries when she hit the instrument panel, but she journeyed on to New York, where she was welcomed as another heroine of the Atlantic crossing.

Amelia Earhart, having established herself as a top pilot in various races with her Lockheed Vega, announced that she intended to fly solo across the Atlantic. Expenses were paid by her now-husband, George Putnam, who not incidentally was publisher of her increasingly profitable books. On May 20, 1932, she took off from Harbour Grace in fair weather. Soon her altimeter failed, and then she was forced to fly through a turbulent electrical storm. Ice formed on the plane's wings, forcing her to drop to a lower altitude, and the exhaust manifold cracked, allowing blue flames to leap out. Worse yet, when she switched on the reserve fuel tank, one of the gas lines began leaking. She realized then that it would be foolhardy to press on to Paris. Setting a course for Ireland, she landed safely in a field in the north, near Londonderry, where she was mobbed by an ecstatic crowd **(opposite, bottom)**. Despite all the problems, her fifteen-hour flight across the ocean was the fastest yet.

In 1935 Amelia Earhart set her sights on making an around-the-world flight. Soon a consortium of corporations gave her a twin-engine Lockheed Electra suitable for long-distance flying **(above)**. The Electra was fitted with extra fuel tanks to give it a range of 4,000 miles, and Fred Noonan signed on as navigator. They took off from Oakland, California, on March 17, 1937, and made their first stopover in Hawaii. On takeoff for Howland Island two days later, the Electra ground-looped and crashed. The aircraft had to be shipped back to Lockheed for rebuilding. Within two months, on May 21, the Electra took off from Oakland again, this time headed east to Miami; Earhart had decided to make the long, dangerous flight over the Pacific her last lap. After takeoff from Miami on June 1 **(below)**, the flight went smoothly, with stops at Brazil (Natal), West Africa (Dakar), and intermediate points in Africa and Asia. Earhart and Noonan left New Guinea for Howland Island on July 2—and disappeared without a trace. Ever since that time, many futile searches have been made, and many rumors and speculations have been put forth and debunked, but the whereabouts of Amelia Earhart, her navigator, and her airplane remain a fascinating mystery

FLIGHTS TO MANY LANDS

On both sides of the Pacific there was great interest in being the first to fly across the vast ocean—on average, about three times wider than the Atlantic. An experienced Australian aviator, Capt. Charles Kingsford-Smith **(left)**, raised enough money to purchase a Fokker trimotor, which he named the *Southern Cross* **(below).** His first major flight began in Oakland, California, on May 31, 1928. He stopped in Hawaii and Fiji before landing in Brisbane, Australia, on June 10. The next year he successfully flew his plane from London to Australia. His next challenge was to fly the Atlantic, nonstop, from east to west.

On June 24, 1930, Kingsford-Smith and his crew—Evert Van Dyck, John Stannage, and J. P. Saul—took off in the *Southern Cross* from a beach near Dublin, Ireland. Not surprisingly, they fought head winds all the way across the Atlantic, and as they neared Newfoundland they became lost in unfavorable weather. Fortunately, they had a good radio. After circling for several hours, they picked up a radio beam that enabled them to find their way to Harbour Grace, where they landed in fog **(above)**. The next day they flew on to Roosevelt Field, New York, and an uproarious welcome from a crowd of about 20,000. Copilot Van Dyk was hailed as he climbed out of the cockpit **(right)**. The *Southern Cross* had become the first plane to cross the Atlantic and make its final stop in the U.S.

In 1928 Bellanca produced a radically new type of plane for transatlantic flight: It was a sesquiplane, a biplane with the bottom wing shorter than the top wing. It had a retractable landing gear and was powered by a Pratt & Whitney Hornet engine **(above)**. The aircraft was built for Cesare Sabelli, an Italian ace who had gained the support of several Italian-Americans for a nonstop flight from the U.S. all the way to Rome. Sabelli, seen at Roosevelt Field (second from right in photo) **(below)**, and his copilot, Roger Q. Williams, barely got their heavily loaded *Roma* into the air from Old Orchard Beach, Maine, before trouble developed and they were forced back to earth. They landed safely but immediately quit the effort, and the airplane was repossessed by Bellanca.

French army pilots Jean Assolant and Rene Lefevre, backed by Armeno Lottis, were also among those who attempted the Europe-to-America flight. They took off from Le Bourget in their Bernard monoplane, the *L'Oiseau Canari* ("The Yellow Bird") on September 4, 1928, but were forced to abort the flight in Casablanca. Subsequently they decided to ship their airplane to Long Island to prepare for the less dangerous west-to-east flight, jumping off from Old Orchard Beach, Maine. There **(right)** Lottis (right) met with rivals Lewis Yancey and Roger Q. Williams. The final takeoff from the beach on June 13 almost ended in disaster when the surprisingly tail-heavy aircraft barely cleared the seawall. Safely in the air, they checked the tail and found the extra weight—a stowaway. With the increased fuel consumption caused by their passenger, the pilots figured that it would be impossible to fly all the way to Paris. They headed for the coast of Spain, where they landed safely. Lottis, Assolant, and Lefevre good-naturedly let the stowaway accompany them to Paris to share in their welcoming ceremonies.

Undeterred by the failure of his projected flight with Cesare Sabelli, Roger Q. Williams tried again, teamed up with Lewis Yancey and a new Bellanca named the *Green Flash* **(below)**. They took off from Old Orchard Beach just minutes after the Frenchmen in their *Yellow Bird*. Unfortunately, one of the Bellanca's wheels was snapped off when it hit a water pocket in the sand, dumping the plane on its nose. Climbing out of the wreckage, Williams and Yancey lived to fly another day.

They bought another Bellanca, the *North Star*, originally intended for Thea Rasche, and renamed it *Pathfinder* **(above)**. As they prepared for takeoff, on July 8, 1928, a representative from the *Daily Mirror* handed them a wreath to drop at sea in memory of the downed *Old Glory* **(below)**. They made it all the way to Spain before lack of fuel forced them to land. After refueling, they flew on to Rome, where they were met with a tumultuous welcome.

Transatlantic fever also struck a number of immigrant Americans, who fancied the idea of flying across the ocean to their places of birth. Otto Hillig, a German, teamed up with a pilot named Holger Horiis, a Dane, to make the big trip in a Bellanca named *Liberty*, for the town in New York State where Hillig lived. After fitting out at Floyd Bennett Field **(opposite, top)**, they flew to Newfoundland, crossing lower Manhattan en route **(opposite, bottom)**. They took off from Harbour Grace on June 24, 1931, and endured a grueling thirty-two-hour flight through fog and turbulence, with Horiis continuously at the controls. They finally spotted an opening in the clouds and landed in a field near Krefeld, Germany. The next day they flew on to Copenhagen and a welcome home for Horiis.

There was a political motive to the flight by Alexander Magyar and George Endres. They planned to fly from America to Budapest, Hungary, in order to direct the world's attention to injustices suffered by Hungarians in the partition mandated by the Treaty of Trianon, after World War I. Hungarian-Americans who supported the flight raised sufficient money to buy a Lockheed Sirius, which was then given the name *Justice for Hungary* **(above)**. Leaving from Harbour Grace on July 15, 1931, Magyar and Endres had a relatively smooth crossing before they ran out of fuel and were forced to land just twenty-six miles short of Budapest. Quickly making their way to the city, they were welcomed by a crowd of about 200,000 cheering Hungarians.

In 1931 another attempt was made to set the long-distance record for a nonstop flight. On July 29, John Polando **(top)** and Russell Boardman took off from Floyd Bennett Field in their J-6-powered Bellanca, which they had named *Cape Cod*. They battled fog and wind over the Atlantic but made it all the way to Istanbul, Turkey, with less than a gallon of fuel to spare. The two exhausted pilots did indeed set a distance record—5,014 miles—in a forty-nine-hour flight. The plane was returned to the U.S. and renamed the *Clevelander*, seen here in 1935 **(bottom)**. Just minutes after the *Cape Cod* left Floyd Bennett, it was followed down the runway by a Bellanca named *Miss Veedol*, for the oil company sponsoring the flight. The pilots, Clyde Pangborn and Hugh Herndon, did fairly well until they got lost over Ireland, eventually being forced to land in Wales, far short of any kind of distance record.

Warsaw was the goal of several transatlantic fliers. Polish emigre aviator Stanislaus Hausner **(right)** set out from Newark, N.J., on June 3, 1932. His plane was a Bellanca named *St. Rosa Maria,* seen here at Floyd Bennett Field **(below)**. Halfway across the ocean Hausner saw that his fuel was leaking. He scouted the shipping lanes for a passing steamer but spotted none before he was forced to ditch. The Bellanca floated well, and Hausner survived for a week before finally being rescued by a British ship.

Not so lucky was Francesco de Pinedo, who had been dismissed from his post as Air Minister of Italy by Benito Mussolini. He acquired a Bellanca monoplane **(above)** and made plans to regain his prestige by breaking the record for nonstop, long-distance flight by flying from New York to Baghdad. On September 2, 1933, Pinedo's *Santa Lucia*. rolled down the runway at Floyd Bennett Field, overloaded with 1,000 gallons of fuel. Unable to lift off in time, the plane ran off the runway, flipped over, and caught fire. Rescuers were unable to reach de Pinedo, and he died in the flames. His plane **(below)** and his dreams were destroyed.

Two brothers from Brooklyn, Joseph and Benjamin Adamowitz, were also determined to fly to Warsaw, their native city. They purchased the *Liberty*, which had already crossed the Atlantic, piloted by Holger Horiis. They had the plane reconditioned and renamed it *City of Warsaw*, then posed in front of it before taking off from Harbour Grace on June 29, 1934 **(above)**. The intrepid brothers flew part of the way across the ocean through gale force winds, which forced them far south of their original route. They finally landed in France, refueled, and soared on to a boisterous welcome in Warsaw.

Cesare Sabelli, standing at the right beside his Bellanca **(opposite, top)**, had never given up on his goal of a nonstop flight from New York to Rome. He named his plane *Leonardo da Vinci* and engaged George Pond as pilot. They took off from Floyd Bennett Field on May 24, 1934, and flew entirely on instruments to Ireland, where engine trouble forced them to land in a field near Dublin. In this photo **(opposite, bottom)** Pond (left) and Sabelli contemplate the sea as they wait for repairs to be completed. More engine trouble forced them to land in England for a complete overhaul, so they did not reach Rome until June 11. Hoping to have a better flight back to North America, they left Rome on August 18. The two ran into heavy fog and crashed into a mountainside in Wales. Both men survived, but their plane was demolished.

On June 22, 1935, two Portuguese brothers, Alfred and George Monteverde, attempted to take off from Floyd Bennett Field in an overloaded Bellanca they had named *Francisco de Pinedo* in honor of their fallen Italian colleague. Unfortunately, the plane met the same fate as its namesake, failing to lift off with its heavy load. It rolled into a sandpile at the end of the runaway **(above)**, but the brothers were lucky enough to walk away with only minor injuries.

Two more entrants in the transatlantic derby were Stanley Girenas (left) and Stephen Darius (right), here waving from the Bellanca they named *Lituanica* **(above)**. They had bought the aircraft with funds raised from people who were mostly Lithuanian-Americans, like themselves, by offering to have painted on the fuselage the names of contributors of $25 or more. On July 15, 1933, they and their plane were at Floyd Bennett Field when Wiley Post took off on his round-the-world flight. Inspired, the brothers gassed up the *Lituanica* and prepared for takeoff. After a mile run, they made it into the air and over the Atlantic. They got as far as Koenigsberg in East Prussia when they ran into powerful thunderstorms. They crashed in a pine forest, and the next morning their bodies were recovered from the wreck. A day of national mourning was declared in Lithuania.

Undaunted, people raised sufficient money to purchase a new Lockheed Vega **(below)** for Felix Waitkus **(above)** to fly on the same route. The *Lituanica II* took off from Floyd Bennett Field on September 21, 1935. Waitkus survived head winds and icing over the Atlantic, in the process using far more fuel than had been estimated. He crash-landed in Ireland and completed the flight a few days later in another aircraft.

Norwegian-American businessmen Thor Solberg (left) and Carl Petersen (right) persuaded the Enna Jettick Shoe Company to sponsor their flight from New York to Norway **(above)**. They took off from Floyd Bennett on August 23 and ran into snow and fog approaching Newfoundland. After circling in the dark for hours, they crash-landed in Darby Harbor and were quickly picked up by nearby fishing boats. Three years later Solberg was back at Floyd Bennett, in a Loening amphibian he named *Liev Eriksson* **(below)**. With another pilot, Paul Oscanyan, he took off on July 18, 1935, but was more cautious this time. They made four intermediate stops before landing in Bergen, Norway, on August 16.

Toward the end of the transatlantic craze, one of Eastern Airlines' best pilots, Dick Merrill, decided to make a round trip flight just to prove how easy and safe it had become. Along with Broadway entertainer Harry Richman, Merrill took off in Richman's new Vultee, *Lady Peace,* from Floyd Bennett on September 3, 1936 **(above)**. The wings were packed with ping pong balls for added buoyancy in case of an emergency landing on the ocean. En route to London, Merrill made it as far as Ireland, but then got lost and landed in a cow pasture. The landing was a good one, so the plane was refueled and they continued on to London, then Paris. The return trip home was going well until they landed in Newfoundland, in what they thought was a smooth meadow. Like Alcock and Brown, they found that what looked like a good level field was in fact a watery bog, and the plane quickly got stuck in the mud. With the help of local people they were able to dig out the plane and continue on their way to New York.

The last civilian transatlantic flight ended like many of its predecessors—in tragedy. The pilots were two Brooklyn youths, Alex Loeb and Dick Decker. Loeb posed in front of their plane, an old Ryan Brougham they had named *Shalom,* at Roosevelt Field **(below)**. On August 11, 1939, they took off from North Sydney, Nova Scotia, headed for Palestine. They never arrived and were presumed lost at sea.

WILEY POST AND OTHERS

In the 1920s an adventurous oil worker named Wiley Post learned to fly and eventually became the pilot for a wealthy Oklahoma oilman, F.C. Hall. Post developed a strong rapport with Hall as they flew to and from various oil properties in the plane, a Lockheed Vega named the *Winnie Mae* for Hall's daughter. Soon Hall was allowing Post to use the Vega for other purposes, such as entering (and winning) the 1930 National Air Races. In 1931 Post got the go-ahead for a much bigger project, flying around the world. He selected Harold Gatty to accompany him as navigator. The two men, Gatty at left slightly behind Post, posed in front of the *Winnie Mae* before the flight **(above)**.

They took off from Roosevelt Field on June 23, 1931, and stopped at Harbour Grace, **(above)**, where the ground crew hand-started the propellor before they flew across the Atlantic almost totally blind. After landing at an RAF airfield in Chester, England, they barreled on to Hanover and Berlin in Germany, then on to Moscow, four stops in Siberia, Nome and Fairbanks in Alaska, and Edmonton, Alberta, before coming home to Cleveland and, finally, Roosevelt Field. Elapsed time: 8 days, 15 hours, 51 minutes—a record. Post soon acquired the plane from Hall and had it repainted with the names of all the places the plane had landed on the historic flight **(below)**. On July 15, 1933, Post set off on another round-the-world flight in the *Winnie Mae*—this time alone, with a Sperry Automatic Pilot. From Floyd Bennett Field he flew nonstop to Berlin, then on across Europe and Siberia, Alaska and Canada, and back to Floyd Bennett, setting another record: 7 days, 18 hours, 49 minutes. According to Post, he slept only about twenty hours during the flight. Two years later Post and folk humorist Will Rogers lost their lives when the *Winnie Mae* crashed in Alaska.

In 1932 Scotsman James Mollison became the first ever to make a solo flight from Europe to North America, flying a small DeHavilland Puss Moth he had named *The Heart's Content* **(above)**. He took off from Port Marnock, Ireland, on August 18, 1932. Like his predecessors, Mollison fought head winds and difficult weather, but he made it to New Brunswick, where he refueled, then flew on to New York. Although he had planned to make a round trip, Mollison called off his return because of extreme exhaustion—and because of the pleas of his bride of three weeks, an aviator named Amy Johnson **(left)**.

In 1933 the Mollisons planned to be the first husband-and-wife team to make the east-to-west crossing. For this effort they obtained a twin-engine biplane, a DeHavilland Dragon Moth, added the obligatory extra fuel tanks, and named it the *Seafarer*. They left southern Wales on July 22, 1933, and took turns at the controls as they flew through head winds and fog **(above)**. Just a bit short of their ultimate destination, Floyd Bennett Field, after thirty-nine hours aloft the Mollisons decided to land at the small airport in Bridgeport, Connecticut. The *Seafarer* touched down just short of the runway and flipped over in a salt marsh. Neither of the Mollisons was seriously injured, and the Bridgeport city officials, grateful for the publicity, renamed the airport in their honor. In 1936, after the Mollisons had separated, James decided to make one more transatlantic crossing. On October 29, 1936, he struck out from Harbour Grace in a twin-engine Bellanca he had named *Dorothy*, after his new flame, actress Dorothy Ward. The two are seen here together in the aircraft **(below)**, but she did not make the flight with him. Once aloft over the Atlantic, Mollison climbed to a high altitude above the bad weather and went full throttle. He landed at Croydon Aerodrome 13 hours and 17 minutes later, a new record.

George Hutchinson was a publicity-wise aviator who often took his family on flying tours of the U.S. In 1932 he obtained a twin-engine Sikorsky amphibian that he planned to fly to London, with his family on board. While waiting for takeoff from Floyd Bennett Field, the Hutchinsons willingly posed for many photos (above). The family dog also went along as they began their transatlantic flight on August 23, 1932, with a crew of four. Their aircraft was named *City of Richmond*, in honor of the home of several financial backers. On September 11 they took off from the west coast of Greenland, heading for Angmagssalik on the east coast. En route, a fuel leak forced Hutchinson to land on the ocean and taxi up on an isolated, somewhat forbidding beach. The family's matching outfits did not include Arctic gear, but after two days they were rescued by a British trawler drawn by what seemed to be a fire on the shore. The Hutchinsons had been shooting off flash bulbs in hopes of attracting the attention of passing ships. Family and crew survived their ordeal in good shape, but the riskiness of their journey made many people take a second look at transatlantic stunt flights. Although the family went on to have some success as a vaudeville act called the Flying Hutchinsons, the major effect of their flight was to end government support of flights by individuals who chose to take more risks that the rest of the world could countenance.

In 1933 Mussolini's Fascist government in Italy sponsored a mass flight across the Atlantic that was nothing like anything that had been seen before. Air Minister Italo Balbo **(right)** led the flight of twenty-five Savoia-Marchetta SM-55X twin-engine, twin-hulled flying boats. The idea was to fly to the Century of Progress Exposition in Chicago and demonstrate the scope of Italian air power. The aircraft were manned by eighty pilots and crew members, who prepared for takeoff from the harbor at Orbetello, north of Rome, on July 1, 1933 **(below)**. They flew to Amsterdam, where one plane crashed (with no casualties), then went on to Ireland, Iceland, Labrador, New Brunswick, Montreal, and Chicago. After a few days they flew east, to Floyd Bennett Field and Jamaica Bay, New York **(opposite, top)**. The planes' unique design, and the spectacle of the air fleet at anchor **(opposite, bottom)**, drew many aviation enthusiasts and other tourists to the site. On August 8 they began the return trip to Italy; one more S-35 crashed on arrival in the Azores. Again, the crew survived, and the mass flight was deemed to be a great success.

LINDBERGH REDUX

Charles Lindbergh's history-making 1927 flight marked the beginning of many journeys to points all around the world. In the summer of 1931 he and his wife of two years, Anne Morrow, flew north and then west on the Great Circle route to Japan and China. For this flight Lindbergh modified the Lockheed Sirius he had purchased in 1930, adapting it for landings on water by replacing the wheels with large aluminum floats and installing a more powerful (575-hp) Wright Cyclone engine. Seen at the College Point, Long Island, facility of the EDO Corporation **(above)**, with the Lindberghs in the foreground, the Sirius was a state-of-the-art aircraft, complete with a sliding canopy and drift lines on the tail for judging wind speed and direction.

In 1933, to escape the publicity onslaught that followed the kidnapping and death of their baby, Anne and Charles decided to fly the Sirius north and east to Europe. In early August they crossed the desolate interior of Greenland, carrying all their own emergency equipment. There were no facilities on the ground, but Anne maintained radio contact with the outside world throughout the trip. They stopped over at Angmagssalik **(opposite, bottom)**, a tiny settlement where an Eskimo boy painted "Tingmissartoq" on the plane's nose **(above)**. (The word meant "the one who flies like a big bird," and the Lindberghs kept it as the name of their aircraft.) They made their way across to Denmark, then down to the Azores and West Africa and back across the Atlantic to Natal, Brazil. This was longest, most dangerous leg of the flight, but they had no trouble. From Brazil they flew north, making a number of stopovers. Their last port of call was the Dominican Republic, from whence they flew directly to the Pan American Airways base near Miami. They were welcomed home to the U.S. on December 16 **(below)**.

DIRIGIBLES

While the intrepid pilots of small planes were flying across the Atlantic in cramped cockpits with few amenities, many others were making the trip in relative luxury aboard the early lighter-than-air ships—dirigibles. In the early 1920s the Zeppelin Company, recovering after Germany's defeat in the World War I, produced the ZR-3, an advanced-design aircraft, for the U.S. Navy. Originally designed to use hydrogen in her giant balloon, she was converted to use helium for the navy. Renamed the *Los Angeles*, the airship made a successful transatlantic crossing in 1924, landing at Lakehurst Naval Air Station **(above)**. She was finally scrapped in 1939.

In 1926 public funds were raised in Germany for the construction of another Zeppelin, known as the LZ-127 or *Graf Zeppelin*. The ship was launched in 1928 from a base near Lake Constance, where this photo was taken **(opposite, top)**. But for the Graf and the Dornier DO-X flying boat, the scene could be from a 17th-century painting. The year after launch the *Graf* began an around-the-world flight sponsored by William Randolph Hearst and his sensation-mongering newspaper empire. On August 7, 1929, the craft took off from Lakehurst and, after stops at Germany, Japan, and Los Angeles, returned to base with a new round-the-world speed record—21 days, 7 hours, 34 minutes. The *Graf Zeppelin* continued in transatlantic service, carrying up to thirty passengers and a crew of the same number. The size of the huge ship can be seen close up in this photo of the ground crew preparing to walk her out of the hangar at Friederichshafen **(opposite, bottom)**.

94

The British government entered the airship derby with the construction of two new ships, the R-100 **(below)**, built by Vickers, and the R-101, built at a government plant. The idea was to improve transportation between the home country and the far-flung colonies. The R-100 made one transatlantic crossing, from England to Montreal, July 29-August 1, 1930. The big ship was scrapped after the R-101 crashed in flames on a hillside in France on its way to India. "What time does this *place* get to Europe?"—Dorothy Parker's arch query about a huge ocean liner—was equally apt for the British airships. Passengers relaxing in the two-story lounge and dining area on the R-100 had little sense that they were cruising through the air at speeds up to 100 mph **(opposite, top)**. The Germans' *Graf Zeppelin* also placed strong emphasis on luxurious accommodations and first-class service. Meals as sumptuous as on any transatlantic liner were served on the finest china, and every table was decorated with fresh flowers **(opposite, bottom)**.

As the technology of lighter-than-air travel advanced, the Zeppelin works continued its program of building bigger and better airships. In 1936 the LZ-129, the *Hindenburg*, was launched and began keeping a regular schedule of crossing the Atlantic in two and one half days—the ocean liner record at this time was a little over four days.

Airships were almost as large as steamships, so that it took a ground crew of hundreds to make one fast on land **(above)**. The *Hindenburg* had been designed to use helium to inflate its huge balloon, but the main source of the gas, the United States, refused to sell the increasingly bellicose Nazi regime any commodity that would help in Germany's military buildup. So the giant airship was converted to use hydrogen, a gas that had one drawback: It was highly flammable. On May 6, 1937, the *Hindenburg* arrived over Lakehurst and prepared to land **(below)**. Shortly after this photo was taken the ship burst into flames during an electrical storm **(opposite)**. Amazingly, sixty-one of the ninety-seven passengers and crew on board survived the disaster, but the days of traveling across the ocean by airship were over.

Around the World and Other Feats

One of the many people bitten by the round-the-world flight bug was a Detroit millionaire named Edward Schlee. He bought a single-engine Stinson Detroiter, named it *City of Detroit*, and engaged airmail pilot Bill Brock as captain. They took off on August 27, 1927, from Harbour Grace, Newfoundland, after Schlee had paid to have the airstrip improved from its virtual cow-pasture status. They arrived safely at Croydon Aerodrome twenty-three hours later, then refueled and took off for Munich, Belgrade, Istanbul, Rangoon, Hong Kong, Hanoi, and Tokyo. At all of these stops they belied the public image of the weary, oil-stained pilot by stepping out of their craft in spotless suits and white shirts **(opposite)** — Brock (left) and Schlee (right) looked like businessmen who had flown into town for a meeting. In Tokyo, friends and officials importuned them to cancel the hazardous flight across the Pacific. Eventually, they gave in and finished the trip aboard ship.

Theatrical producer John Henry Mears bought a Fairchild FC-2 that he planned to take around the world, flying over land and packing it aboard ship for the transoceanic travel. Mears and pilot Charles Collyer, with the aircraft Mears named *City of New York*, sailed for England on June 28, 1928. All in all, they had a successful trip, making it around the world in 23 days and 15 hours. The *Graf Zeppelin* soon broke this record, as noted previously, but Mears was undaunted. He then bought a Lockheed Vega, *City of New York II* **(above)**, and vowed to fly across the by-now-well-traveled Atlantic in order to make the trip in better time. The producer and a new pilot, Henry Brown, set off from New York and landed at their jump-off point, Harbour Grace. On August 3, 1930, hoping to save time, they chose to begin their Atlantic hop in the dark. Unfortunately, the Lockheed swerved off the runway and into a ditch. Though neither man was hurt, their trip was over, never to be resumed.

It wasn't long before two more fliers **(above)**, Hugh Herndon (left) and barnstormer Clyde Pangborn (right), laid plans to overturn the *Graf Zeppelin*'s record. Before they had a chance to take off in their Bellanca, named *Miss Veedol* after the oil company that was backing them **(below)**, Wiley Post and Harold Gatty returned from their round-the-world flight with the record that would hard to beat. Herndon and Pangborn then decided to save time by flying nonstop all the way to Moscow, but they got lost over the Atlantic and were forced to land in Wales. They continued on to Siberia, but by that time it was clearly impossible for them to beat Post and Gatty's time, so they gave up.

James Mattern (above, left) and Bennett Griffin (above, right) also decided to go for the around-the-world record. In a Lockheed Vega similar to Post's *Winnie Mae*, they took off from New York (Floyd Bennett), refueled in Harbour Grace, and sped to Berlin fully ten hours ahead of Post and Gatty's time. Mechanical failure then intervened, however, when a hatch blew off and damaged a tail fin. They made a forced landing in a peat bog near Minsk, where the plane flipped over. Undeterred, Mattern had the aircraft repaired for another try, this time alone. With his plane now painted to resemble a giant eagle (below), he took off alone from Floyd Bennett on June 5, 1933, bound for Paris. Ice formed on the wings over the Atlantic and forced him off course. He eventually came down in Norway, refueled, and flew on to Moscow, leaving there five hours ahead of Post and Gatty's time. But then his engine failed over Siberia, and he made a forced landing on the tundra. After wandering in the trackless waste for several days, he was rescued by Eskimos. Mattern never tried again.

The last great round-the-world flight before World War II was made by the flamboyant multimillionaire Howard Hughes in a Lockheed Super Electra he personally bought and fixed up with advanced instrumentation. The flight was made as part of the publicity for the New York World's Fair, but Hughes paid for everything, including the airplane, himself. With a hand-picked crew—Hiram Thurlow, Harry Cannon, Richard Stoddard, and Edward Lund—and with pomp and ceremony befitting a movie mogul **(above)**, he took off from Floyd Bennett on July 10, 1938. In constant touch with weather stations around the world, Hughes never deviated more than six miles from this carefully plotted course. Landing at Paris, Omsk, Yakutsk, Fairbanks, and Minneapolis, the *World's Fair* returned to New York in 3 days, 19 hours, 17 minutes, cutting Post's record in half. After the 14,824-mile-long flight, Hughes (center) and the crew were honored with the traditional New York ticker-tape parade **(right)**.

In 1933 the French government commissioned construction of a large single-engine monoplane in hopes of setting a new record for a nonstop flight from New York across the Atlantic. Like Lindbergh's *Spirit*, the *Joseph Le Brix* was something of a flying gas tank, carrying 1,800 gallons of fuel. It had no windshield on its cockpit, thus reducing wind resistance but eliminating any forward vision for its pilots and giving the aircraft a most unusual look **(above)**. Designed by the famed aviator Louis Bleriot, the experimental aircraft was shipped to New York and prepared for flight at Floyd Bennett Field. Pilots Paul Codos and Maurice Rossi took off on August 5, 1933, and landed in Rayak, Syria, after a record-breaking flight of 5,900 miles. They tried for another record in 1934, taking off from Le Bourget and heading west. The aircraft's wing developed major problems with vibration, perhaps because of the weight of another fuel tank added to increase capacity of 2,055 gallons. The only choice was to dump some of the fuel, continue across the Atlantic, and terminate the flight at Floyd Bennett Field. Nevertheless, Rossi (left) and Codos (right) received a big welcome in New York **(below)**, and their names went into the record books as the first to fly nonstop across the Atlantic in each direction.

One of the longest-lasting flights across the Atlantic was made by one of the largest flying boats ever launched, the German Dornier DO-X **(above)**. The triple-deck flying palace, with a wingspan of 157 feet and grossly underpowered despite its twelve Siemens-Halske engines, in 1929 took off on a test flight with 169 people on board—easily breaking the record for the most people airborne in one aircraft. In 1930 big Curtiss Conqueror engines replaced the Siemens-Halske machines. In November the DO-X embarked on a trip across the South Atlantic, making a call at England en route to Lisbon. Mishap followed mishap. Soon after takeoff the big bird was forced down at sea and had to taxi sixty miles to a harbor in France. A fuel tank caught fire in Lisbon, and it was a month before repairs could be made. The DO-X was damaged attempting to take off from the choppy waters off the Azores, thus losing another three months to repairs. Finally, on June 4, 1931, with Captain Friedrich Christiansen in command, the DO-X began its flight across the Atlantic, stripped of all extraneous weight. Still, the behemoth could rise no more than about thirty feet above the water all the way to Brazil. After stopping at many ports of call in South and Central America. the DO-X arrived in New York Harbor on August 28 **(opposite, top)**. Drydocked at North Beach, Queens **(opposite, bottom)**, the site of present-day LaGuardia Airport, the DO-X had greater success as a tourist attraction than it ever did as a revenue airliner before returning to Germany in May 1932.

The last remarkable flight of the transatlantic pioneer days was made by Douglas Corrigan **(above)**, an impish aircraft worker who had helped build the *Spirit of St. Louis* at the Ryan plant on the west coast. An aviator at heart, he bought a used Curtiss Robin in 1938 for $325 (about six weeks' pay). He painted it silver, prepared it for a long-distance flight, and named it *Sunshine* **(below)**. After some bureaucratic problems with licenses from the U.S. Dept. of Commerce, he took off from Long Beach, California, on July 8, 1938, headed east. He landed near New York with four gallons of fuel to spare. The next week he moved his old plane to Floyd Bennett Field and prepared it for another long-distance flight—he claimed—back to the West Coast. On July 17, at 5 A.M., he took off and was last observed heading east. According to Corrigan, he flew almost entirely through clouds and fog. After several hours he discovered fuel leaking into the fuselage, but solved the problem by poking a hole in the fabric and letting the liquid drain off. After a flight of just over twenty-eight hours, he landed—to his "surprise," not in California, but in Ireland. Thus, "Wrong Way" Corrigan made headlines, giving the world a welcome laugh and catapulting Corrigan into celebrity status, complete with a ticker-tape welcome home back in New York **(opposite)**. He sold his autobiography and the movie rights to his flight for a hefty $75,000, which he used to buy an orange grove back home in southern California, happily outside the public spotlight.

COMMERCIAL SUCCESS

In the late 1930s Germany, France, and Great Britain engaged in many survey flights, testing the feasibility of commercial airline service across the Atlantic—as well as the military implications of such flights. Because of the relatively short range of the flying boats available, a number of early flights were completed in two stages, imitating, in primitive fashion, the way the space shuttle is launched into orbit. The Short Company of Great Britain developed a composite system whereby a small flying boat piggybacked on a larger aircraft, then was launched into independent flight while the mother ship turned around and returned to base. The Germans developed a similar system. Here the seaplane *Nordmeer* is catapulted from the converted freighter *Schwabenland*, off the Azores **(opposite, top)**, to fly north across the Atlantic to Pan American's base at Port Washington, New York **(opposite, bottom)**. The German planes, carrying the Nazi swastika, made eight flights of this type in 1936, fourteen in 1937, and twenty-eight in 1938, all without serious incident. In July 1937 a British Imperial Airways flying boat named *Cavalier* made a successful flight from Foynes, Ireland, to Port Washington **(above)**. The next year another British aircraft, the *Mercury*, flew to Port Washington **(below)**, having been launched over the Atlantic by a flying boat, which then returned to England.

In August 1938 a French Latecoeur flying boat, *Lieutenant de Vaisseau Paris*, flew from Bordeaux to Port Washington **(above)**, with one stop in the Azores. Also in August the Germans surprised the world with an unannounced non-stop flight from Berlin to New York, which took about twenty-five hours. This was the second successful point-to-point flight from Europe to the U.S. (Costes and Bellone in 1930 had piloted the first). The plane was a four-engine Focke-Wulf Condor named the *Brandenburg* **(below)**, piloted by Capt. Alfred Henke. The plane returned to Berlin on August 13, in a flight that took just under twenty hours.

Pan American Airways also made numerous survey flights across Atlantic, beginning in July 1937 with a nonstop flight carrying mail to Foynes, Ireland. Here the crew members, under the command of Capt. Harold Gray, are being rowed ashore at their next stop, Southhampton, England **(above)**. The first commercial passenger flight across the Atlantic took off from Port Washington, New York, on May 20, 1939, bound for the Azores. The distinguished roster of passengers included Juan Trippe, the aviation pioneer who was Pan American Airways president. The four-engine Boeing 314 *Yankee Clipper*, shown here at takeoff **(below)**, had a wing span of 152 feet and a cruising speed of 184 mph. Separate sleeping, dining, and recreation compartments for the seventy-four passengers were located on two levels.

Within a few months Pan Am moved its operations much closer to the heart of New York City, the new Marine Air Terminal on Flushing Bay, in Queens **(opposite)**. The historic, round Art Deco building at the terminal is still in operation, although it no longer draws crowds of sightseers like this group watching a clipper get ready for departure **(above)**. To the regret of historians, none of the glorious Boeing flying boats — not even the fabled *China Clipper* — was preserved for posterity.

"The year will surely come when passengers and mail
will fly every day from America to Europe."

— CHARLES LINDBERGH, 1927

INDEX